What can you see and do at Kew?

Useful plants

Plant survival

Climb and scramble
amongst the **Treehouse
Towers** - suitable for 3-11
year olds. Play in **Climbers
and Creepers** if you are
9 years or younger.

Kew around the world

Be a badger in
our human-sized
Badger Sett.

Become an explorer

Palm House

Inside the Palm House, it is like
the steamy tropical rainforest.

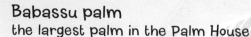

Did you know?
The Palm House has 16,000 panes
of glass. No wonder it takes
weeks to clean them all!

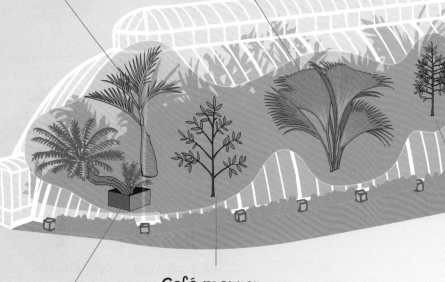

Babassu palm
the largest palm in the Palm House

Panama hat plant
see Plants and
People Exhibition

**Cacao
tree**

Bottle palm
see Plants in danger

Coco-de-mer

Annatto tree

Coffee bush

**Coconut
palm**

**Vanilla
orchid**

Café marron
see Plants in danger

Cycad
Kew's oldest pot plant

Giant
bamboo

Put a sticker next to each plant on the list that you spot on your jungle jaunt.

Mango tree
only produces fruit in the tropics

Sugar cane

Rattan palm

Banana
look for green
unripe bananas

Marine
Display

Rubber
tree

Find the plants

Annatto tree

Rattan palm

Cacao tree

Rubber tree

Coffee bush

Coco-de-mer

Cycad

Sugar cane

Giant bamboo

Vanilla orchid

The pond is this way.

You can find out about these plants on the next few pages.

Inside the Palm House

Find rainforest plants that are ingredients for some of the world's favourite foods and drinks.

Chocolate, yum!

Cocoa pods grow from the trunk of the cacao tree. The pods contain cocoa beans. The beans are collected and piled up. This makes them warm and wet and brings out their chocolate flavour. They are then dried out and transported to chocolate factories.

Cacao tree

Cacao beans

Coconut mat

Curries, cakes and doormats

Coconuts are the seeds of the coconut palm. The white kernel inside is used in many foods from curries to cakes. The coarse fibres on the outside of the coconut can be made into doormats.

Coconut

Curry

Coconut palm

Annatto or bixa tree.

Food colouring

The orange colour in many foods comes from the soft flesh that surrounds the seeds of the annatto tree. In tropical America, native people use the colour as body paint and lipstick.

CHEESE

Did you know?
A coconut can kill, if it falls on a person's head!

4

Ice-cream flavour

Vanilla flavour comes from the seed pods of this tropical climbing orchid. The pods have no flavour until they are sweated and dried. Natural vanilla is expensive so most vanilla flavouring is artificial.

Vanilla orchid

How many ants can you see on this page? Answer at the back of the guide.

Wakey, wakey!

Most of the world's coffee comes from tropical America. The plant is a bush which has red fruits. There are two coffee beans inside each fruit. The beans need to be roasted before they smell and taste of coffee.

Coffee bush

Fizzy drinks can have loads of sugar.

Sweet grass

Sugar cane is a tall grass, which grows in the tropics. The canes are shredded and crushed to release the sweet juice inside. Over two-thirds of the world's sugar is made from sugar cane.

Sugar cane

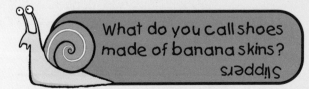

What do you call shoes made of banana skins? Slippers

5

Inside the Palm House

Look for these rainforest plants, which help us to build and make things. You can also find some record-breakers here.

Cutting rattan

Rubber balls

A tapper collecting latex

Cane chairs

Rattans are climbing palms with long stems that are made into cane chairs, baskets and mats. The palm has spines that help it to scramble high in the forest canopy. The spines may hurt collectors harvesting rattans from the rainforest.

Rattan

Bouncy balls

White liquid, called **latex**, oozes from cuts made in the bark of the rubber tree. The latex is dried and made into stretchy rubber. Balls made of rubber bounce because they spring back into shape.

Rubber tree

Coco-de-mer

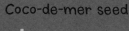
Coco-de-mer seed

Big bum

The Coco-de-mer palm has the world's largest seed, whic looks like a big bottom. The seed weighs up to 30 kilos. After a seed thuds to the ground, it takes over two yea before it starts to grow.

Triceratops

Giant bamboo

Really ancient

Cycads are a group of plants that thrived 200 million years ago, when dinosaurs liked to eat them! This cycad in the Palm House is over 200 years old.

The cycad is Kew's oldest pot plant.

Fast grass

Giant bamboos are the world's fastest growing plants. They grow up to 25 metres high, which is as tall as a stack of 16 cars. Bamboo is used for scaffolding in south-east Asia because it is strong and flexible.

Bamboo scaffolding

I'm a rainforest pitcher plant. Unscramble the words to find plants you might need if you got lost in the rainforest without supplies.

Clue — all the plants are on the Palm House map!

1. Make a shelter using **alpm** leaves and **omobab** poles.
2. Take cane from the **tartan** palm to make a chair.
3. Collect some **tonococus**, **sanbnaa**, **asrgu neca**, and **esnoamg** to eat.

Answers at the back of the guide

Palm House Marine Display

Head downstairs in the Palm House to discover plants that live on the shore and in the sea.

Coral reef

Some tiny plants are partners with animals, called corals. They help the corals build huge reefs in tropical seas. Coral reefs are home to many kinds of fishes and other animals. Most reef fishes are brightly coloured to signal to others on the crowded reef.

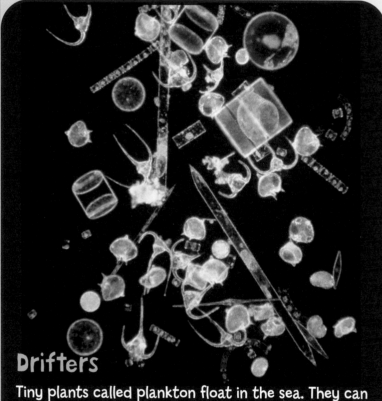

Drifters

Tiny plants called plankton float in the sea. They can only be seen with a microscope. Plankton make much of the oxygen we breathe. They are also food for small floating sea creatures which are eaten by fish. The blue whale, the largest animal on Earth also eats plankton.

Mangrove swamp

Mangrove swamps are found mostly in the tropics where fresh water mixes with salt water. The mangrove shrubs are partly submerged when the tide comes in. Prop roots anchor the plants in the mud.

British estuary

Estuaries are where rivers meet the sea. In cooler parts of the world, such as Britain, salt marshes are found in estuaries. Plants growing in the mud bind it together and help to protect the coast.

Rocky Shore

Have you seen a rocky shore when the tide is out? You can spot sea plants called seaweeds. Different types of seaweed are different colours. They look like an underwater forest when the tide is in and the water covers them.

Why is the sand wet? Because the seaweed!

My snail cousins live at the seaside. Please colour in the seaweeds on their menu.

1. Sea lettuce — I'm green. I live where fresh water runs down the shore.

2. Irish moss — I'm red. I live in rock pools and low down the shore. I am eaten in bramble flan in Ireland.

3. Kelp — I'm brown. I live low down the shore and in deeper water. Jelly taken from my leafy fronds keeps your ice cream soft.

9

Plants and People Exhibition

Discover more useful plants and some beautiful and bizarre things made out of plants.

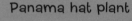

Panama hat

Cool hats

Hats made from dried leaves keep you cool in summer. The largest hat on display is made from leaves of the coconut palm. The panama hat shows how strips from the leaves of the hat plant are woven together.

Panama hat plant

Cannibal Cutlery

This fork and plate from the Fijian islands are made of wood from the intsia tree. They were given to Kew in the mid 1800s when fortunately the practice of eating people was coming to an end.

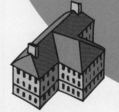

Museum No 1

Poisonous plants

People in the Amazon rainforest coat their arrows and blow-darts with different poisons. The poisonous roots of a vine are sometimes used for arrows. A drug made from this poison was also used to relax a patient's muscles during surgery.

Quiver for poison arrows

You would not be here without plants! We give you oxygen, food, shelter, medicines, clothes, and more.

Heart pills

Chemicals from foxgloves have been used in heart medicines for over 200 years. You can find foxgloves growing in the Conservation Area in summer.

You can see a coconut palm and panama hat plant in the Palm House.

Ancient Scroll

The stalks of papyrus were made into a material to write on in Ancient Egypt. The papyrus plant grows in wet places in tropical Africa, including along the river Nile.

Papyrus scroll

Why did the tomato blush?

Because he saw the salad dressing.

Can you pick the correct answers to these questions about the Plants and People Exhibition?

1. What item of clothing on display is made from pineapple leaves?
   a. socks **b.** shirt **c.** pants **d.** jumper

2. What plant produces a seed case, which you can use to scrub your back?
   a. sponge **b.** bottle-brush plant **c.** prickly pear **d.** loofah

3. Half the world eats the seeds from which kind of grass?
   a. rice **b.** corn **c.** bamboo **d.** rye

4. Wood from which tree is used to make cricket bats?
   a. oak **b.** sycamore **c.** pine **d.** willow

5. What plant dyes your jeans blue?
   a. blackberry **b.** indigo **c.** blueberry **d.** strawberry

6. What poisonous seeds are made into jewellery?
   a. rosary **b.** deadly nightshade **c.** lupin
   d. golden rain tree

7. What part of plants belonging to the cucumber family can you play music with?
   a. leaves **b.** roots **c.** gourds **d.** flowers

   Answers at the back of the guide.

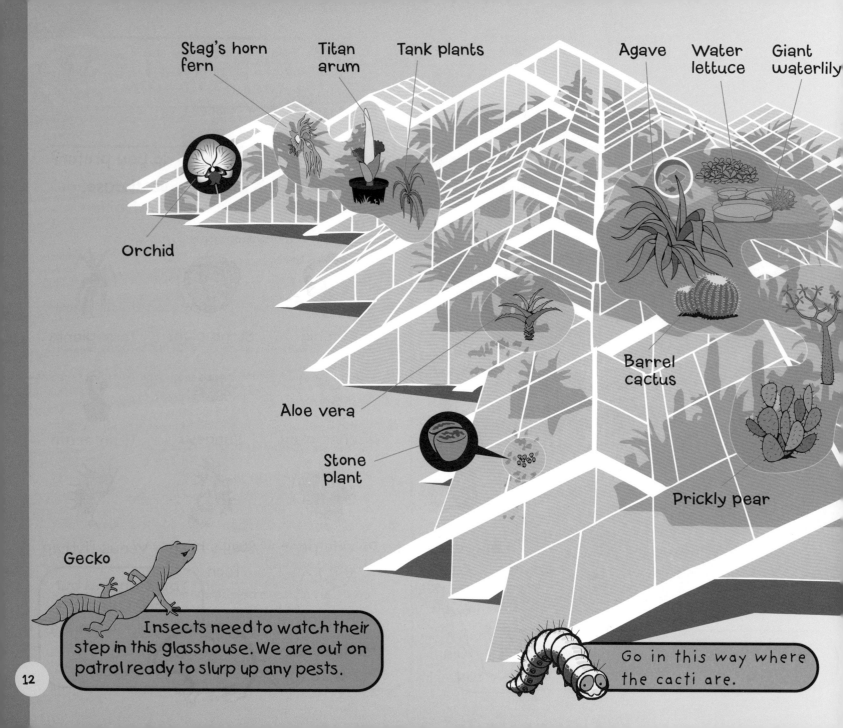

Stag's horn fern

Titan arum

Tank plants

Agave

Water lettuce

Giant waterlily

Orchid

Barrel cactus

Aloe vera

Stone plant

Prickly pear

Gecko

Insects need to watch their step in this glasshouse. We are out on patrol ready to slurp up any pests.

Go in this way where the cacti are.

Pitcher
plant

Sundew

Venus
flytrap

Madagascan
tree

Princess of Wales Conservatory

Warm, wet or dry - which tropical climates do you prefer?
You will find many climates in this amazing glasshouse.

Put a sticker next to each plant on the list that you spot on your walk around the desert and rainforest.

Find the plants

Agave

Orchid

Stone plant

Tank plants

Aloe vera

Pitcher plant

Sundew

Titan arum

Barrel cactus

Prickly pear

Stag's horn
fern

Venus flytrap

Giant
waterlily

Madagascan
tree

You can find out about these plants on the next few pages.

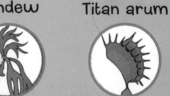

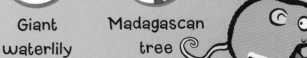

13

Inside the Princess of Wales Conservatory

Seek out plants that grow in deserts and other dry places.

Barrel cactus

Watery insides

The barrel cactus grows in American deserts, where it can survive for long periods of time on its store of water. The thick waxy outer layer keeps the water in and acts like sun-block.

Living stones

Stone plants look like stones, which may help them escape the notice of animals that might eat them. These plants grow in South Africa's drylands. When stone plants flower after the rains, they are much easier to see.

Stone plants

Madagascan tree

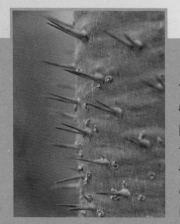

Madagascan tree spines

Spiny trunk

This unusual tree comes from the dry forests of Madagascar. The spines on the trunk collect moisture from dew. It drips onto the ground then is sucked up by the tree's shallow roots.

Peel me first

The fruits of the prickly pear are covered in sharp spines. By carefully peeling the fruits, people can eat them. The orange flesh inside is also made into sweets.

Prickly pear

Did you know?
Conservatory is another name for a glasshouse.

Lookalike

Agaves look rather like aloes but they come from the other side of the world. Agaves live in dry places in Mexico, south-western USA and Central and South America. Each circle or rosette of leaves only flowers once, then dies.

Agave

Say aloe

Aloes come from Africa and Arabia. They survive in dry places by storing water in their thick leaves. The jelly-like liquid from the leaves of aloe vera soothes the skin.

Aloe vera

Aloe vera lotion

Do you have shampoos or lotions made of aloe vera in your bathroom?

Cactus
Stone plant
Prickly pear
Agave
Aloe

Fit the plant names into the puzzle.

P r i c k l y p e a r
c a c t u s
A L o E
s t o n e p l a n t
A g a n e

Answers at the back of the guide.

Inside the Princess of Wales Conservatory

Enter the lush wet zone where you may encounter giant leaves and flowers.
Explore more to see orchids and ferns.

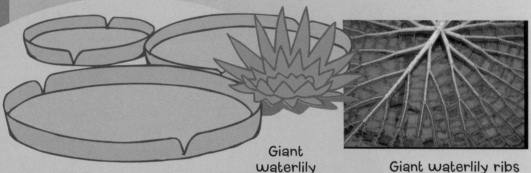

Giant waterlily

Giant waterlily ribs

Water lettuce

Waterlily wonder

Giant waterlily leaves can grow over two metres across in summer. The leaves float because they trap pockets of air between the ribs underneath. The ribs are armed with spines to keep fish from nibbling at them.

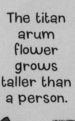

The titan arum flower grows taller than a person.

Lettuce menace

The water lettuce grows at the surface with its roots hanging down into the water. In some places, such as Florida in the USA, it is a menace. The dense growth blocks the light, and kills underwater plants.

The floating leaf can take the weight of a baby. Please do not try this yourself!

A single giant leaf grows up afer the flower dies back.

Big stink

You may see the titan arum in bloom in summer. It is the biggest flower in the world and smells foul. The flower grows up from a huge corm (a type of bulb). The titan arum comes from the Sumatran rainforest in Indonesia.

Bromeliads on trees

Perfect pools

Tank plants perch high up on rainforest trees. The leaves collect water to make a little mid-air pool in which frogs sometimes raise their tadpoles.

Tank plant or bromeliad

Showy orchids

Orchids have many beautiful flowers. Their seeds are tiny and blow away in the wind like dust. Most tropical orchids grow on tree branches, where their dangling roots catch moisture from the air.

Fabulous ferns

The stag's horn fern grows on branches in the rainforests of south-east Asia. It is too high up to get nutrients from the soil. Instead, the fern collects debris in its leaves.

Stag's horn fern

Fern waterfall

Orchid on a tree

Tropical orchid

Inside the Princess of Wales Conservatory

Discover plants that digest animals, and go down the ramp to see who is underwater.

Have fun with us monsters in Climbers and Creepers.

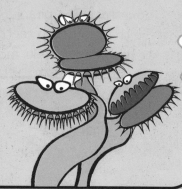

Sundew

Stickers

Sundews have droplets of glue to trap insects – just like flypaper. In some sundews, the leaf slowly wraps around the struggling victim to suffocate it. The dead insect is then digested.

What goes 99-bonk, 99-bonk, 99-bonk?

A centipede with a wooden leg.

Feed me

Carnivorous plants need to digest animals because they live in boggy places, where there are not enough nutrients in the soil. These meat-eating monsters have cunning tricks to trap small animals – most of which are insects.

Venus flytraps also digest spiders.

Snap trap

An insect feeds on nectar at the base of the teeth but when it brushes against trigger hairs several times the leaf snaps shut. The teeth interlock to prevent the insect escaping. The leaf squeezes the insect and starts to digest it when still alive.

18

Slip and Slide

An insect is lured deep inside a pitcher plant by large helpings of nectar. The deeper it goes, the more slippery the wall becomes. The insect slips and tumbles into the liquid at the bottom where it drowns and is digested.

Small animals, such as frogs, sometimes fall into large pitchers and get digested too.

Pitcher plant

Piranha fish

Nasty nashers

You can see a piranha in one of the smaller tanks downstairs. The piranha has powerful jaws armed with razor-sharp teeth that rip out chunks of flesh. Fortunately, most kinds are shy of people.

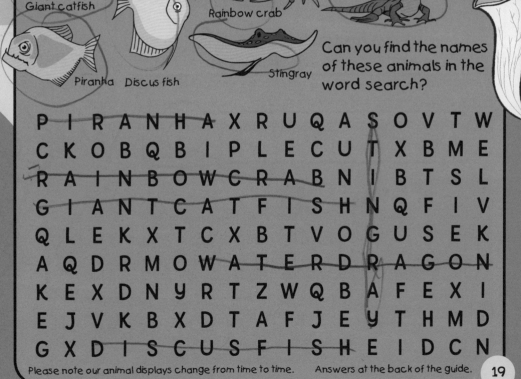

Giant catfish

Piranha   Discus fish

Rainbow crab

Stingray

Water dragon

Can you find the names of these animals in the word search?

```
P I R A N H A X R U Q A S O V T W
C K O B Q B I P L E C U T X B M E
R A I N B O W C R A B N I B T S L
G I A N T C A T F I S H N Q F I V
Q L E K X T C X B T V O G U S E K
A Q D R M O W A T E R D R A G O N
K E X D N Y R T Z W Q B A F E X I
E J V K B X D T A F J E U T H M D
G X D I S C U S F I S H E I D C N
```

Pacu

If you look in the waterlily pond you can see pacu. These fish are related to the piranha but prefer to picnic on fruit and nuts.

Please note our animal displays change from time to time.   Answers at the back of the guide.

19

Spring at Kew

You can see millions of flowers, such as crocuses, daffodils, and bluebells.

Glory of the snow
April

These flower after the snow melts in their mountain homes in Turkey, Crete and Cyprus. They are also called *Chionodoxa* - say *chee-ono-dox-a*.

Crocuses
February to March

Crocuses grow from bulbs, called corms, which are swollen stems whereas daffodil bulbs are swollen leaves. Over one-and-half million crocuses bloom in the Crocus Carpet near the Victoria Gate.

Crocus

Daffodils February to March

Daffodils are bred for their colour, shape and scent. Wild daffodils grow in the woodlands and mountains of Europe including Britain. Like many spring bulbs, daffodil bulbs are poisonous, which stops animals eating them.

Daffodil

Bluebells
April to May

The British bluebell is at risk from cross-breeding with the Spanish bluebell, which has spread from gardens. You can spot a British bluebell because its flower stem droops to one side.

British bluebell

wildlife watch

Visit the ponds and lakes to find these baby wild water birds.

Coot with young

Mallard ducklings

Why do ducks watch the news?
To get the feather forecast.

What do I carry from flower to flower so that they can make seeds? Fill in the puzzle to see the answer in the shaded squares.

1. When are tulips in bloom?
2. What kind of bulb is used with cheese to flavour crisps?
3. What part of a plant is green and traps sunlight?
4. What do bees do to get around quickly?
5. What chocolate treats do you eat in spring?
6. What is the name of the sweet substance in flowers?

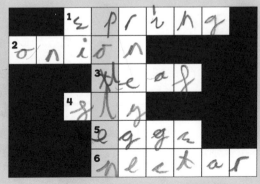

1. spring
2. onion
3. leaf
4. fly
5. eggs
6. nectar

Answers at the back of the guide

Summer at Kew

On a warm summer's day why not bring a picnic and sit under the shade of the trees?

Roses

June to August

Just like bees, we are attracted to roses by their scent and colour. We can make perfumes from roses, and even a scented jam out of rose petals.

Rose

Bamboos

all year

You can see bamboos different shapes and si in the Bamboo Garden One of the Chinese bamboos in the Garden is the only food giant pandas eat.

Lavender
July to August

Lavender comes from the Mediterranean region across to India. They do not need much water so are good plants to grow when we have water shortages and a ban on using hosepipes in the garden.

wildlife watch

Look for butterflies around flowers that are rich in nectar. Find damselflies and dragonflies around the lakes and ponds.

Painted lady butterfly

Blue-tailed damselfly

Emperor dragonfly

Summer gardening tips

Plant lettuce seeds in your garden or container outside. Keep the soil damp, and seedlings will appear about a week later. Soon you will be picking delicious lettuces.

Sunflowers

June to August
Look for sunflowers in the Gardens. If it is a good summer, they can grow taller than you.

Sunflower

What do insects learn at school?
Mathematics!

23

Autumn at Kew

The leaves of many of our trees change colour. You can see fruits, nuts, and mushrooms.

Sweet chestnut

Inside the green prickly fruit are two to three shiny chestnuts that are delicious when roasted. The ancient Romans were probably the first to grow sweet chestnut trees in Britain.

Sweet chestnut tree - one of the oldest trees in the garden.

Sweet chestnut

Ginkgo

The female tree sprouts seeds that smell awful when they rot. If you pick up the seeds from the ground, their sickly smelling goo may irritate your skin. A stinky female tree is marked on the map.

Ginkgo leaves   Smelly ginkgo seeds

Gingko

Japanese maple

The leaves of the Japanese maple in the Woodland Garden turn yellow with orangey edges. The bark of the young branches is a reddish orange.

Pampas grass

Look for pampas grass in the Grass Garden. This South American grass grows bigger than an adult person. It has large feathery seed heads.

Pampas grass

Why did the mushroom go to the party?

Because he was a fun guy to be with.

Wildlife Watch

Spot squirrels and jays carrying off acorns to hide. Look for pine cones gnawed by squirrels to get at the seeds inside. Be careful not to touch the mushrooms in case they are poisonous.

Poisonous fungi

Squirrel

Jay

25

Winter at Kew

Wrap up warm and take a brisk walk around Kew's winter wonderland.

Holly

A good crop of holly berries is thought to mean a hard winter ahead. In fact, it means the summer weather was good so that many flowers set seed. We have over 56 different kinds of holly on Holly Walk.

Only female holly trees have berries.

Holly

Viburnum
October to March

You can smell the pink flowers from several metres around the Ice House. In the 1700s ice cut from ponds was stored in the Ice House. The ice was used in summer to keep food and drinks cool.

I spend most of the winter asleep in my sett.

Viburnum

Witch hazel
December to February

The curly yellowy-orange petals look like a burst of sunshine on a cold winter's day. Extracts from the bark and leaves are used to treat bumps and insect bites.

Snowdrops

January

Snowdrops are some of the first flowers to bloom at the end of winter. Wild snowdrops grow in Britain across Europe to Turkey.

Snowdrop

Wildlife watch

Times are hard for birds in the winter months. They may have to find food under the snow.

Robin

Canada geese

What does a caterpillar do on New Year's Day? Turns over a new leaf!

Plant explorers

For over 200 years people from Kew have travelled the world in search of plants.

Beginning with Banks

Sir Joseph Banks (1743–1820) was a friend of George III and an intrepid explorer. Banks sent the first plant hunters from Kew on expeditions to bring back rare and useful plants.

Sir Joseph Banks

Sir Joseph Dalton Hooker

Rhododendrons

In the Himalayas

Hunting for new kinds of rhododendrons in the Himalayas was gruelling for Sir Joseph Dalton Hooker (1817–1911), who became head of Kew. He was infested with 100 blood-sucking leeches after tramping the foothills.

The marvellous Miss North

Marianne North (1830–1890) was a plant explorer and artist. She came from a rich, well-connected family. When she was young she met lots of her father's friends, including Sir William Hooker, then Director of Kew Gardens.

Travelling the world

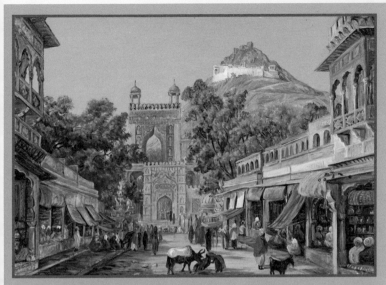

For 14 years Marianne travelled to many countries including Japan, India and Australia. In the days before widespread travel and photography her landscape paintings gave people a rare glimpse of these far-away places.

Painting places and plants

Marianne worked hard on her travels. Amazingly, she produced over 800 oil paintings. These show all kinds of plants growing in fields, forests, on mountains, by rivers, near the sea. Many are of plants close up, showing their flowers and fruits.

Discovering unknown species

Some plants Marianne painted were unknown to the experts at Kew and elsewhere. A few of these were later named after her. This one is called *Nepenthes northiana*.

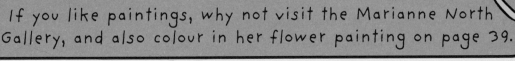

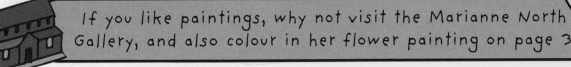

If you like paintings, why not visit the Marianne North Gallery, and also colour in her flower painting on page 39.

Become an explorer

Take a trek around the Gardens to track down some terrific trees.

Scramble up the Xstrata Treetop Walkway for an exciting view. Discover what lives around tree roots in the Rhizotron.

Xstrata Treetop Walkway

Climb 118 steps to walk amongst the treetops. Every season brings new views of our trees. High above the ground, you can see far into the distance.

California giants

The coast redwood is the world's tallest tree towering over 115 metres. The giant redwood is the biggest with a trunk measuring 31 metres around. Redwoods take hundreds of years to reach record sizes. Our trees are youngsters with the oldest planted in 1912.

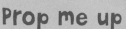

Giant redwood

This Japanese pagoda tree actually comes from China!

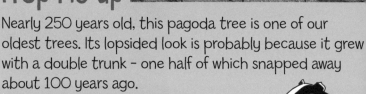

Prop me up

Nearly 250 years old, this pagoda tree is one of our oldest trees. Its lopsided look is probably because it grew with a double trunk – one half of which snapped away about 100 years ago.

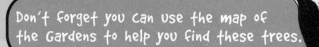

Don't forget you can use the map of the Gardens to help you find these trees.

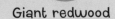

Big puzzle

The monkey puzzle tree comes from Chile and Argentina in South America. The tree got its name when first grown in England because a person joked it would be hard for a monkey to climb.

Monkey puzzle tree planted in 1846.

The oak's leaf has tooth-like edges like a sweet chestnut leaf.

Chestnut-leaved oak

What a whopper!

The chestnut-leaved oak is Kew's biggest tree. It was planted in 1846. The tree grows over 30 metres tall and the branches spread 30 metres across, which is nearly three times the length of a London bus.

How many trees grow at Kew?
a. 700 **b.** 5000 **c.** 8900 **d.** 14,000
Answer at back of the guide.

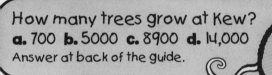

Unlucky tree

A small plane flew into the top of this tree in the early 1900s. Since then it has been struck by lightning twice. You can see the split in the bark left after it was struck in 1992.

Corsican pine planted 1814.

Wollemi pine

Still living

Scientists thought the Wollemi pine became extinct two million years ago. In 1994 pines were discovered living in a gorge near Sydney, Australia. Kew is helping to grow more Wollemi pines because there are so few in the wild.

31

Become an explorer

Watch out for wildlife up in the trees, in the water and hidden under rotting logs.

Take a wildlife walk in the Conservation Area

Smelly heaps

We make our own compost from dead and waste plants, and truckloads of horse manure from the army and police stables. On cold days, the gigantic piles of compost steam because they get so warm from the rotting plant matter and dung.

Be a badger

Explore the tunnels in the human-sized badger sett we have built at Kew to show how badgers live.

Wildlife friendly

We look after wildlife at Kew. You can see all sorts of birds in the Conservation Area. Have a go at a pond dipping session at the Dipping Pond.

I go out looking for food when everyone has gone home to bed.

Meet the tree gang

The tree gang are expert at climbing trees. They use ropes and pulleys like mountain climbers. They have to saw off branches that might otherwise fall on your head.

Stag beetle sculpture in the Loggery

Stag beetle heaven

The Loggery is made of rotting logs, home to the grubs of Britain's largest beetle, the stag beetle. The grubs spend over four years feasting on the rotting wood before turning into adults.

How many of my mini-beast friends are living in the log pile?

Woodlouse   Millipede   Centipede

Ground beetle   Earwig   Stag beetle grub

Answers at the back of the guide.

Kew does not use peat because digging for peat destroys the boggy places where sundews like me grow.

33

Buildings old and new

Visit some beautiful old buildings.
Witness the latest in glasshouse design at Kew.

Kew Palace

This royal palace was once the home of George III. He spent time here as a child in the school room, and also when he fell ill with a disease that made him seem mad.

These buildings are on the map of the Gardens. Use the coloured boxes on this page to help you find them.

Queen Charlotte's cottage

Did you know Kew was home to tigers as part of the Royal Family's collection of animals in the early 1700s?

Royal cottage

The thatched cottage was given to Queen Charlotte when she married George III. The Royal Family had picnics here. Kangaroos and exotic birds were once kept nearby.

Bombs away

This Chinese-style pagoda was built in 1762 for George III's mother. At that time it had 80 golden dragons perched on the roofs. In World War II bomb designers dropped dummy bombs from the top floor to test them.

The Pagoda

We are Japanese

Our Japanese Gateway is a much smaller copy of one in an ancient city in Japan. Can you see the gateway's beautifully carved flowers and animals? Stroll around the gateway to see what gardens look like in Japan.

Minka

Recycled house

The Japanese Minka is a house made of wood. It has a thatched roof and mud plastered walls. This traditional style house was taken apart in Japan and rebuilt here. Minkas withstand earthquakes, which are common in Japan.

Amazing paintings

See flower paintings old and new at the Marianne North Gallery and the Shirley Sherwood Gallery of Botanical Art.

At what time does a duck wake up?

At the quakc of dawn.

Plants in danger

More and more plants are at risk as forests are chopped down, and wild places are taken over by towns and farms.

Time for trees

Much of the dry forest on the coast of Peru in South America has been cut down for farming and fuel wood. We are working with local people to plant more huarango (say wa-ran-go) trees.

Children help to plant trees in Peru.

Our world may be getting warmer because of people's energy-guzzling lifestyles. Plants like me may die out.

Seed bank saviours

Over a billion seeds from around the world are kept safe at Kew's Millennium Seed Bank at Wakehurst Place. We are collecting and storing seeds from places where plants are at risk, and we are helping other countries to set up their own seed banks.

By 2020 we hope to have a quarter of the world's different kinds of wild plants saved in the Seed Bank.

Jungle adventures

Today, Kew helps people around the world to look after their plants. Expeditions to the rainforest in Cameroon, West Africa aim to discover which plants there are under threat.

Wild food

Kew's scientists are looking at traditional foods in Africa, such as roasted seeds from the sausage tree. Traditional foods may help people in Africa stay healthy and find enough to eat in times of famine.

The sausage tree is named for the shape of its fruit - not because it grows sausages!

Bottle palm

This palm only grows wild on Round Island, Mauritius in the Indian Ocean. In the 1970s, it almost died out because rabbits and goats like to eat it. Seedlings from Kew have been planted back in the wild.

You can see the bottle palm in the Palm House.

Some of our rarest plants are grown in the laboratory.

Which plant lives where?
Match the plant to where it lives

Harebell

Desert

Rocky shore

Stag's horn fern

Cactus

Grassy meadow

Rainforest

Seaweed

Answers at the back of the guide.

Colouring fun

Colour in this dragon from the Japanese Gateway. Can you find a dragon in front of the Palm House?

Follow in Marianne North's footsteps and colour in her painting of the sacred lotus from Java. Go to page 28 to read about her adventures.

Puzzling fun

Can you help me back to my hive?

How do bees get to school?
On the school buzz!

START

40

Hello, I'm a sundew. Can you help me spot five different things in the pictures below? The white box is a sticky trap like me that catches insect pests.

Join the dots to find out who is lurking in the Palm House pool.

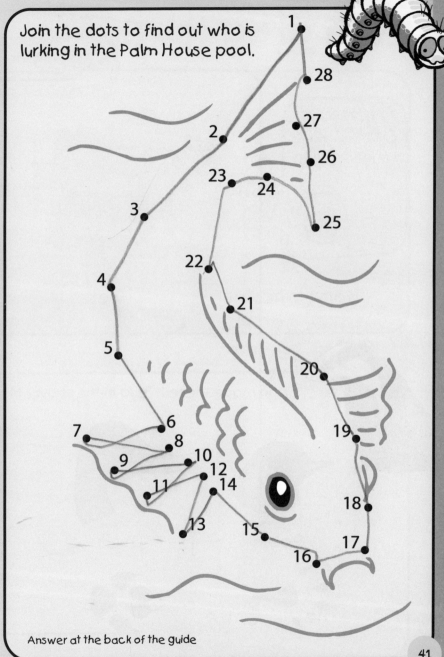

Activity fun

Horse-chestnut   Oak   Pine   Ash

Answers at the back of the guide.

Who made these tracks in the snow? Match the animal with its tracks.

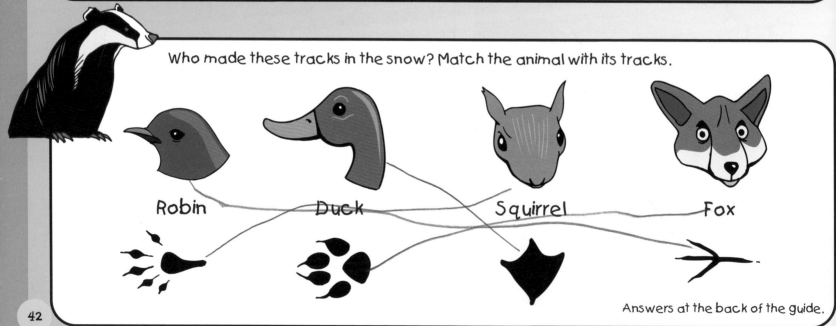

Robin   Duck   Squirrel   Fox

Answers at the back of the guide.

Grow a hyacinth

Wear gloves if you have sensitive skin.
Balance a hyacinth bulb on top of a
narrow jam jar full of water. The roots
will grow to fill the jar.
The bud opens into
a scented flower.

Plant an oak tree

Pick up an acorn and plant it
in a pot outside.

Your baby oak should sprout
in spring. When it out-grows
the pot, you can put it in a
larger container.

Grow a Sunflower

If you want tall sunflowers in your
garden or container in summer, you
can give them a head start by
planting seeds in small
pots indoors in spring.

43

Make a bark rubbing

Bark is the outer layer of woody plants including trees. The colour and pattern of the bark can help you identify a tree. To make a record of the pattern take a rubbing of the bark.

You will need:
- strong paper
- wax crayons or chalk

Place your paper on the bark. Rub the crayon or chalk lengthwise across the paper.

Bark rubbing

Make a pine cone animal

Olly Owl

Use your imagination to make cone animals such as birds, mice, etc.

You can find pines cones lying on the ground around the coniferous trees in parks and other gardens. Please collect only what you need.

Dinosaur garden

You will need:

- a washing-up bowl
- a bag of gravel
- attractive stones
- peat-free potting compost
- bottle-garden plants (you can buy them in garden centres)
- toy dinosaurs

Put 5—6 cm of gravel in the bottom of the bowl. Then fill it to within 1 cm of the brim with potting compost.

Create a cave, valley or cliff and prehistoric landscape with the stones, then position the plants. When you're satisfied with how it looks, plant your little bottle-garden plants.

Release your dinosaurs, letting them, and your imagination, roam.

Pressed flowers

Have fun pressing garden flowers.
You will need:

- flowers from your garden
- some old newspapers
- several sheets of kitchen or blotting paper
- a stack of heavy books

Pick flowers when they are dry (no rain or dew). Pansies and poached-egg plants press well. With fat flowers like roses and poppies, it is better to press individual petals.

Place an old newspaper on a table and put kitchen or blotting paper on top. Arrange your flowers on the paper. Cover with blotting or kitchen paper. Top off the pile with another newspaper and a stack of heavy books. Leave your flowers to dry for two weeks.

Use pressed flowers to make cards or pictures, or stick them on to paper to study. Botanists still dry plants to study like this. A collection of pressed plants is a herbarium — Kew's Herbarium is very big.

REMEMBER Always ask permission to collect flowers or weeds. Don't collect wildflowers, as many are becoming rare.

Here are some things to do at home

I'm a harebell — I live in wild grassy places. You can help wildflowers like me and other wildlife by doing some of these things.

Dig a pond.
Pile up old logs.

Build a bird table and
a bird bath.
Put up a bird or bat box.

In dry summers use
dirty bathwater to
water plants.

Grow wild flowers
to help bumblebees.

Leave grass and nettles to
grow in a sunny place in your
garden as food for caterpillars.

Use a water-butt to
collect rainwater for
watering your plants.

Answers page

Pages 4 and 5
Number of ants on the pages = 32.

Page 7 Word scramble
Make a shelter using **palm** leaves and **bamboo** poles.
Take cane from the **rattan** palm to make a chair.
Collect some **coconuts, bananas, sugar cane** and **mangoes** to eat.

Page 11 Plants and people quiz
1b. shirt, 2d. loofah, 3a. rice, 4d. willow, 5b. indigo, 6a. rosary, 7c. gourds

Page 15 Word puzzle

Page 19 Word search

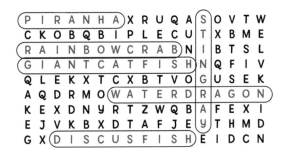

Page 21 Word puzzle

Page 31 Number of trees
d. 14,000

Page 33 Numbers of mini-beasts in the log pile
Woodlouse = 4
Millipede = 3
Centipede = 3
Ground beetle = 4
Earwig = 3
Stag beetle grub = 3

Page 37 Matching game
Harebell lives in **grassy meadow**.
Stag's horn fern lives in **rainforest**.
Cactus lives in **desert**.
Seaweed lives on **rocky shore**

Page 41 Who's lurking in the pool?
Koi carp

Page 41 Spot the difference
mushrooms, pool of water, leaf beside bucket, leaves in bucket, leaf on tree

Page 42 Matching game

My name is Sticker the sundew.

Kew
ROYAL BOTANIC GARDENS

This third edition published in 2014
by the Royal Botanic Gardens, Kew,
Richmond, Surrey, TW9 3AB, UK

Written by Dr Miranda MacQuitty
Illustrated by Guy Allen
Designed by Louise Millar
Development editor: Lydia White

ISBN 978 1 84246 508 0

10 9 8 7 6 5 4 3 2 1

www.kew.org

Printed in Spain by GraphyCems

The paper used in this book contains material
sourced from responsibly managed and sustainable
commercial forests, certified in accordance
with the FSC (Forestry Stewardship Council).

FSC
www.fsc.org
MIX
Paper from
responsible sources
FSC® C007507

The following people have provided invaluable help and advice:
Anoushna and Samuel Aylward, Raffat Bari, Shirley Beadle, Sandra Bell, Fiona
Bradley, Vicky Brightman, Gail Bromley, Karen Brown, Henry and Rose de Chazal,
Colin Clubbe, Lucy Cole, Simon Cole, Louise Cross, Ambar and Hannah Driscoll,
Emily Dutton, Matilda, Jem and Ross Frisby, Gina Fullerlove, Laura Geary, Phil
Griffiths, Christina Harrison, Tina Houlton, Tony Kirkham, Lloyd Kirton, Jane, Emily
and Michael Lambert, Paul Little, John Lonsdale, James and Oliver Morley,
Peter Morris, Mark Nesbitt, Christine Newton, Jill Preston, Sue Seddon,
Varsha, Shivani and Ria Sokal, Katie Steel, Nigel Taylor, Amber Waite,
Catherine Welsby, Lydia White.

We would like to thank the following for providing photographs and for
permission to reproduce copyright material:
Acro Images/Alamy 19; Heather Angel/Natural Visions 8; Jeff Collett/ Natural
Visions 8; Emma Dodd 23, 43, 45; Jan Sevcik 19; Redmond Durrell/Alamy 19;
Jeff Eden 32; Peter Gasson 17, 21, 23, 25; Hemera Technologies/Alamy 11;
Laura Jennings 17; Christabel King 37; Paul Little cover, 1, 5, 8, 10, 20;
William Milliken 37, James Morley cover, 16; Norman T Nicoll/Natural Visions 8;
RBGE/Ian Edwards 7; StockStill/Alamy 21. 25; Oliver Whaley 36; Lydia White
14, 15; all other photographs by Andrew McRobb.

For information or to purchase all Kew titles please visit
www.kewbooks.com or email publishing@kew.org

Kew's mission is to inspire and deliver science-based plant conservation
worldwide, enhancing the quality of life.

Kew receives half of its running costs from Government through the
Department for Environment, Food and Rural Affairs (Defra). All other
funding needed to support Kew's vital work comes from members,
foundations, donors and commercial activities including book sales.

When you find a plant at Kew put a sticker on the plant lists in the guide.

 Corsican pine

 Rubber tree

 Titan arum

 Rattan palm

 Cycad

 Giant waterlily

 Stag's horn fern

 Viburnum

 Daffodil

 Snowdrop

 Monkey puzzle

 Gingko

 Venus flytrap

 Aloe vera

 Giant bamboo

 Pitcher plant

 Stone plant

 Agave

 Sweet chestnut

 Wollemi pine

 Rose

Japanese pagoda tree

Annatto tree

Giant redwood

Tank plants

Can you find the stickers for the trees and other plants you spot in the Gardens?

Crocus

Cacao tree

Barrel cactus

Vanilla orchid

Madagascan tree

Coco-de-mer

Orchid

Sunflower

Sundew

Chestnut-leaved oak

Holly

English bluebell

Coffee bush

Sugar cane

Can you find the stickers for plants you spot in the glasshouses?

Prickly pear